by Judith Herbst

Lerner Publications Company • Minneapolis

Lerner Publications Company
A division of Lerner Publishing Group
241 First Avenue North
Minneapolis, Minnesota 55401 U.S.A.

Website address: www.lernerbooks.com

Library of Congress Cataloging-in-Publication Data

Herbst, Judith.
      Monsters / by Judith Herbst.
           p.   cm. — (The unexplained)
      Summary: Introduces such "monsters" as the Yeti, zombies, and the Loch Ness monster, debunking many of these fantastic stories.
      Includes index.
      ISBN: 0–8225–1626–8 (lib. bdg. : alk. paper)
      1. Monsters—Juvenile literature. [1. Monsters.] I. Title. II. Series: Unexplained (Lerner Publications)
      QL991.H47 2005
      001.944—dc22   2003022691

Manufactured in the United States of America
1 2 3 4 5 6 – JR – 10 09 08 07 06 05

Table of Contents

CHAPTER 1
Bigfoot: It Walks among Us
5

CHAPTER 2
Nessie: It Came from Beneath the Loch
18

CHAPTER 3
I Walked with a Zombie
28

CHAPTER 4
The Swamp Thing and Mothman
36

Find Out More
46

Index
47

"Ahr-r-r-r-r-ruh-uh-uh!"

—The Beast from *20,000 Fathoms*

4

CHAPTER 1
BIGFOOT: IT WALKS AMONG US

It is dark and cool, like the inside of a tomb. Only the exit lights are glowing blood red and far away. The air is overripe with the buttery smell of movie popcorn, the floor sticky with wads of bubble gum and squashed Junior Mints. It is 1967, and Roger Patterson's monster film has just been released. They say it is shaky and crude and only a few minutes long. The lighting isn't very good, and there's no plot. But every ticket has been sold, and every seat is filled.

The projector whirs softly in the little booth above the balcony. The screen blinks a few times as Patterson's short strip of 16-mm film crackles to life. The chattering audience falls silent. This time, they have been told, the creature in the movie may be real.

The film begins, but the picture is blurry. Patterson seems to be running after something, and the camera is jumping in his hands. He loses his footing, and the scene slips away at an odd angle. There is a confusion of color, and then suddenly, the camera finds its subject.

Oh, my gosh! What is that?

The film runs another few seconds and then stops abruptly. The movie is over. The lights come up, but the audience continues to sit in silence, staring openmouthed at the darkened screen.

What had Roger Patterson filmed meandering along Bluff Creek in northern California on that autumn day in 1967? Patterson claimed it was a female Sasquatch (from a Salish Indian word meaning "wild man of the woods") and never wavered from his story. Others insisted it was just a man in a furry suit. Somebody must be right, but who?

Stills from Roger Patterson's and Bob Gimlin's film, taken in 1967, distinctly show some sort of creature walking along the Bluff Creek riverbed and heading into the woods.

It sounds like something straight out of Hollywood on a day when nobody could come up with a good plot idea. A giant, apelike creature stomps around the Pacific Northwest (or the Himalaya mountains in Tibet or the South American rain forest or the African Congo) leaving footprints and scaring the socks off the local residents. A few folks have seen it, and one old codger claims the thing kidnapped him, but most scientists just laugh and think everybody is hallucinating. Or lying. Or having a little fun.

"I agree," says the studio bigwig. "It's hokey and farfetched. That's why I like it. How does it end?"

Oooohh. Good question. We don't know yet. Despite the Native American legends that go back hundreds of years, the woodsmen's stories, and the Tibetan tales, despite the many footprints in mud, snow, and dry riverbeds, this creature continues to elude us. Very few people have ever seen it, and fewer still have gotten any photographs. Nobody has ever captured one. So this bogeyman of the forest, this Abominable Snowman of the mountains, is either one whopper of an imaginary animal—or playing the best cat and mouse game ever staged.

>> Act 1: Bigfoot Gets a Name

It was 1921 when the daring mountaineer Lieutenant Colonel C. K. Howard-Bury led the first-ever expedition to the peak of Mount Everest. As Howard-Bury, five other climbers, and 26 Sherpa guides made their way across Tibet's Kharta Glacier, they came upon an enormous footprint in the snow.

This footprint was photographed in the snow-covered mountains in Washington State by Cliff Crook in February 1996. It measures 14.5 inches long by 7 inches wide. It was obviously made by a big foot . . . but was it Bigfoot?

In this artist's rendition, a Yeti watches from afar as a group of climbers scale a peak in the Himalayas.

The Sherpas knew immediately who—or perhaps what—had made the tracks. "Metohkangmi," they said, pointing. "Also called Mirka, Sogpa. You know? Yeti."

Howard-Bury nodded. "Ah, yes. Yeti, the Abominable Snowman." He snickered at such a ridiculous notion. It was unimaginable to him that a completely unknown race of large, hairy apemen could be living anywhere in the world—let alone way up here, in this icy desolation. "Wolf tracks," he suggested, but the Sherpas shook their heads.

"No. Metohkangmi," they insisted, and crinkled their noses in disgust. Although none of them had actually seen the

LOVE THOSE MONSTERS!

Monsters have been with us a long time. Some of our oldest stories describe the exploits of a brave and usually handsome hero who sets out to slay a loathsome monster. These monsters are as different as the cultures that create them, but nearly all have a few things in common. They are usually large and dwell in inaccessible places, such as thick forests, icy wastelands, or remote mountains. They are almost always ugly. Some combine the traits of several different animals or are a human/animal combination. Finally, monsters must be rarely—if ever—seen but always rumored to exist.

Almost as soon as we learned to take moving pictures, Hollywood began cranking out monster films. The most famous is probably *King Kong*, but theatergoers have also been delightfully frightened by the likes of the *Creature from the Black Lagoon*, *The Fly*, *The Beast with a Million Eyes*, and *Godzilla*.

creature, they all knew about it. It had been part of Tibetan folklore for as long as anyone could remember. Most spoke about its foul smell and its taste for yak, its high-pitched shriek that could be heard echoing through the icy canyons late at night. A true monster, powerful and hulking, secretive and frightening.

"Well, yes, ahem," said Howard-Bury, who brought the story home to England but didn't for one second believe it. Abominable Snowman indeed! Why, anyone could see it was just mythological nonsense. But

This 15-inch footprint was found in northern California the same year that Patterson filmed his Bigfoot movie.

Howard-Bury had heard only the Tibetan version. He probably had no idea that there was also the Sasquatch in Canada, Shiru in Latin America, Muhalu in the Congo, Alma in China, and Orang Pendek in Indonesia, just to name a few. And these creatures were all leaving behind very BIG footprints, which is how this creature—which may or may not exist—got its American name: Bigfoot.

>> Act II: Casting the Part of Bigfoot

The movie director taps his head thoughtfully. "Let's see, now," he mumbles to nobody in particular, "whom can we get to play the part of Bigfoot?" He shuffles some papers on his oversized desk, selects one, and begins reading.

"Bigfoot," he says in a booming voice. "Average height is between seven and ten feet tall. Weighs several hundred pounds. Covered in coarse, dark hair, sometimes reddish in color. Hmmm. Sounds like my father-in-law."

This cone-shaped object covered with fibers or hair is said to be a Yeti scalp.

He chuckles to himself and continues. "Very muscular, heavy neck and shoulders, walks upright but hunched over. Long arms that extend all the way to the knees. The descriptions vary, but he is often described as having a cone-shaped head. No tail. Gives off a terrible, disgusting smell. Geesh! And this guy's going to be the star of my movie? I must be nuts."

The director scans the page and continues to read aloud to an empty office. "The creature is said to leave footprints that measure anywhere from 11 to 22 inches long and as much as 10 inches wide. Makes grunting sounds but can't speak. That's good. At least we don't have to write dialogue for him. Well, now," says the director, leaning back in his fancy leather chair and tapping his upper lip thoughtfully. "I'm thinking that there are maybe three possible creatures who could play the part of Bigfoot. One, the so-called "missing link" between apes and humans. Two, a descendant of the extinct ape *Gigantopithecus.* Or three, some sort of as-yet-undiscovered humanlike creature." His eyes glowing, the movie director bounces forward in his chair and excitedly punches the intercom button. "Greta!" he screams. "Quick! Get me central casting!"

Back when Charles Darwin published his theory of human evolution, a good chunk of the populace was horrified. They thought he had said that humans were descended from apes, which certainly would have made a monkey out of him. But what Darwin had actually said was that if we go back far enough in time, we find that apes and humans arose from a common ancestor. The apes then went one way, and we went the other.

Not everyone agrees with Charles Darwin's theory of evolution. This cartoon from the mid-1800s portrays Darwin himself as half man, half ape.

But when you start with a misconception, you tend to develop goofy theories, which is how the idea of a missing link arose. If, some people reasoned, humans gradually evolved from apes, there must have been a time when we looked more like apes than we do now. This "man-ape" or "ape-human" would supposedly be the missing link. But there is no missing link because, as we have seen, humans did not come from apes. So the suggestion that Bigfoot is one of these prehistoric apemen must go into the shredder.

The next theory is that Bigfoot might be a relative of *Gigantopithecus,* who showed up about seven million years ago. *Gigantopithecus* broke off from the branch of the primate family tree that gave rise to the orangutan, but it was much, much larger than any of those primates. While the average male gorilla stands about 6 feet tall and weighs 400 pounds, *Gigantopithecus* was probably over 10 feet and weighed close to 1,200 pounds. The fact that it had very big feet goes without saying.

One theory of Bigfoot is that he is a relative of *Gigantopithecus.*

Once thought to be extinct, a living coelacanth was found in the Indian Ocean in 1938. The discovery gives hope to people who thought that *Gigantopithecus* might still be lurking in the woods.

Gigantopithecus survived successfully for about 6.5 million years and then became extinct. But could it have living relatives? It's entirely possible. Could science have missed finding them? Certainly. If they are shy, nocturnal, and live in remote parts of the world, they would be very easy to miss. Science was absolutely certain that the coelacanth fish had become extinct about 70 million years ago until a fisherman caught a live one in 1938. What else might be out there waiting to surprise us?

Of course, if Bigfoot does exist, it may not be an ape at all. One theory suggests that the creature is some sort of unknown hominid. (The word "hominid" comes from the Latin root *homo-*, meaning "human.") But to be a hominid, a primate must meet certain requirements. An upright posture, for example. The jaw can't protrude. The thumb has to be opposable (easily able to grip), but the big toe isn't allowed to be. It's a tough club to get into. Does Bigfoot have the right stuff? Let's go to the prop room and see what we can find out.

>> Act III: The Bigfoot Prop Room

You may hear an echo because there's not much here. True to monster form, Bigfoot has left behind very little hard evidence of his existence. You've already seen the film, which may or may not show a real Bigfoot. There are also a few blurry and indistinct photographs and some bits of hair. And, of course, there are the footprints.

The footprints, with their world-famous size and shape, are preserved in plaster for all to see. They look impressive, but are they actual Bigfoot prints?

This may surprise you, but footprints do not always provide the best evidence. Footprints in the snow melt and enlarge. Wind and rain—

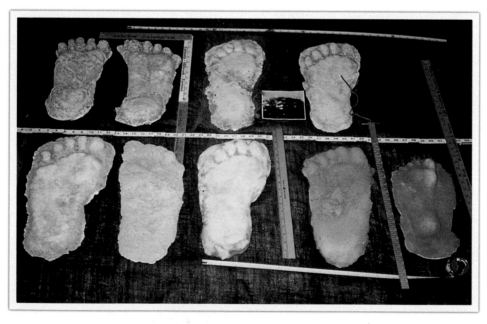

These Bigfoot casts were all taken of footprints found in the Pacific Northwest. The smaller cast on the bottom right is of a human foot.

Bigfoot researcher Cliff Crook examines hair strands found near some footprints. The hair had been wrapped in Native American beads.

even if it's only a drizzle—can quickly distort tracks left in sand and soft mud. So unless you're right there with your handy-dandy plaster cast making kit when Bigfoot walks by, you probably won't get an accurate impression.

However, an intriguing report published in the *Journal of the Idaho Academy of Science* in June 2001 describes unusual skin ridge details—the equivalent of fingerprints—in four sets of casts taken of alleged Bigfoot tracks. "The features," says the report, "are distinct from those of humans. The ridges themselves are wider on average than [those] found in humans and non-human primates."

In other words, the question "Does Bigfoot really exist?" is not yet answered. And what could be a better way to end our movie than that?

CHAPTER 2

NESSIE: IT CAME FROM BENEATH THE LOCH

Hugh Gray was an ordinary guy who was in the right place at the right time. He also had a camera with him.

It was November 12, 1933, a bright, sparkling Sunday. Mr. Gray was taking a walk along the shore of Scotland's Loch Ness when he noticed a great deal of splashing in the water. Oh my, he thought, and snapped a picture. The splashing continued, and from the inky waters of Scotland's largest lake there arose a dark gray shape of "great size," said Mr. Gray. He ook another picture. He didn't see a head but said that "there was considerable motion" from what he believed to be a tail. Mr. Gray continued to take photographs, ending up with five in all before the thing from the loch (the Scottish word for "lake") sank beneath the waves it had so recently created.

Mr. Gray was no doubt disappointed when only one of his pictures came out, but he sent that one precious photograph to Graham Kerr, a professor of zoology at the University of Glasgow, along with a description of the event. Professor Kerr, however, frowned. He did not see a head like a seal or a body like an eel, as Mr. Gray had said. He did not see fins along the sides. In short, he did not see much of anything except, perhaps, "a curved shape in the water," and he seriously doubted that Mr. Gray had photographed a living thing at all.

Early accounts of Nessie date back to around A.D. 500. Some stories portray it as a threatening creature, as depicted in the illustration on the facing page. *Below:* Hugh Gray snapped this photograph of a curved shape in the waters of Loch Ness on November 12, 1933.

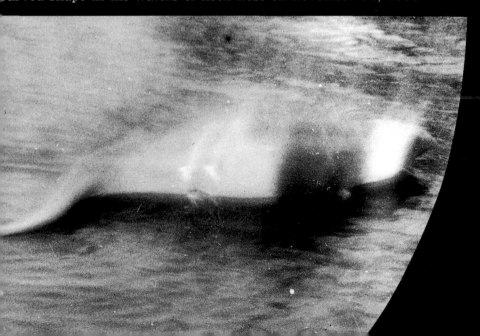

Alex Campbell

But Professor Kerr's opinion didn't matter to the folks who lived around Loch Ness. They had long been convinced that something pretty big was living in their lake. Stories about the creature went back at least a thousand years, and besides, their own Alex Campbell had seen the monster dozens of times.

Alex Campbell had been the game warden at Loch Ness for 45 years. He had also lived on the lake and had grown both familiar and comfortable with its strange personality. So, yes, he could tell the difference between a floating log and, well, something else entirely. Campbell was unshakable in his belief that some kind of prehistoric-looking marine animal was swimming around in the 700-foot depths. He described it as having a small head and a snakelike neck about 6 feet long. He estimated the total length of the creature to be 30 feet.

And this, apparently, is just what London surgeon R. Kenneth Wilson photographed while on holiday at Loch Ness in April of 1934.

The Surgeon's Photograph, as it came to be called, appeared in the following Saturday's edition of London's *Daily Mail* and caused, as you might expect, quite a commotion. "Yes!" exclaimed all the eyewitnesses. "That's what we saw!" Meanwhile, the doubters snorted and insisted that

This photo, known as the Surgeon's Photograph, is one of the most famous—and most disputed—images of the Loch Ness Monster.

the photo had been faked. But amazingly enough, the Surgeon's Photo has held up quite well under scrutiny—despite one strange little episode when doubt was cast upon it.

In the 1990s, a man named Christian Spurling claimed the picture was a hoax and that he had been part of the fun. But his explanation of how the trickery was accomplished didn't wash. It was far-fetched and complicated, involving a 35-mm camera, negatives, positives, and plates. Why not, asked Henry Bauer in the *Journal of Scientific Exploration,* just use a plate camera in the first place? Spurling's claim was further questioned when an alleged coconspirator named Ian Wetherell described a different process altogether. He said that a toy submarine had been used to move the "monster" through the water and create a V-shaped wake. But look closely at the picture. There is no wake. You have to wonder if Mr. Wetherell had even seen the picture that he was supposed to have faked.

>> Nessie Makes a Movie

"Miles! Olivia! Come quick! Nessie's on the telly!"

It was one of the most extraordinary movies ever shown on British television. In 1960 a man named Tim Dinsdale had captured an unidentified something or other with two humps moving through the waters of Loch

In this film still footage
from Tim Dinsdale's movie taken on
Loch Ness in 1960, we can see what could be
Nessie (black spot) moving first left, then right, and leaving
a large wake.

Ness. As several thousand people watched on flickering black-and-white TV sets, Nessie teased and tantalized with her first-ever 16-mm film performance.

And this time, the thing in the loch was leaving behind a wake.

"Wait a minute," said the critics. "Not so fast. The wake could be from a boat."

But the scientists who examined Dinsdale's film didn't think that was very likely. A boat would also leave a different kind of trail, from the propeller. "And take a look at these frames," they said. "See how the water swirls, there and there? It's like a swimmer doing the breaststroke."

"Then here and here," they said, pointing to two stills from the film, "we also see the humps, just visible above the surface of the water. And it's pretty obvious that this thing is submerging. Notice in these frames how the wake narrows and the humps disappear."

The critics snorted. "Maybe that's because it's a submarine."

"Sorry," said the scientists. "Nothing like that was in the loch when Dinsdale shot his movie. You want our opinion? This thing is clearly moving under its own power across the loch. It curves around to the left and then continues parallel to the shore. Look. You can even see little splashes on either side."

The critics' eyes bulged. "You mean it's *paddling?*"

And when the scientists nodded, the critics asked their last question. "Are you saying that this might actually be the Loch Ness Monster?"

"What we are saying," said the scientists, "is that this film shows there is a large, fast-moving creature we have yet to identify living in Loch Ness."

It was a rave review.

>> On Location with Nessie

Does Nessie have a stunt double? It's a fair question. If everybody who ever claimed to have seen the creature saw *the same* animal, then Nessie is one very old beastie, indeed. Even if you don't count the thousand-year-old legends, eyewitness reports go back several centuries at least. Could an animal live that long?

If Nessie is some kind of Jurassic leftover from the Age of Reptiles, then the answer is yes. While paleontologists cannot say for sure how long the dinosaurs lived, their best guess is two to three hundred years, maybe even five hundred. If that's the case, Nessie doesn't need a stunt double.

But there is another possibility. There might be more than one. Intriguing as this may be, it creates a problem. Can the loch support even as few as two Nessie-sized creatures? Let's go on location and find out.

Loch Ness is Scotland's largest freshwater lake, and it is strange indeed. It is 22 times longer than it is wide, and its depth in some places is more than 900 feet. The streams and rivers that empty into the loch carry decaying plant material called peat from the bogs and swamps that they pass through on their way. The thick, gushy peat hangs heavy in the water, making it impossible for sunlight to penetrate the murky depths. Because of the darkness, there are no plants in the loch. So if Nessie actually exists, she is certainly not a vegetarian.

TURTLE TIME

We usually think of animals as having rather short life spans, and compared to humans, most do. But tortoises are the notable exception. Perhaps it is their slow and steady gait or the fact that they are strict vegetarians. Whatever their secret, tortoises live well over 100 years. For example, a giant tortoise from the Seychelles, a group of islands off the African coast, was captured in 1766. It long outlived its kidnappers, finally dying in 1918. The average life span of a giant Galápagos tortoise is nearly 200 years. If a creature such as Nessie exists, it might also enjoy such a long life span, and many sightings over the years could actually all refer to the same beast.

The loch is well stocked with fish, but are there enough to feed two or more animals reported to be as big as railroad cars? Doubtful, say the scientists. Nessie would have to come and go, swimming in and out of Loch Ness and enjoying most of her meals in the North Sea. But for a big monster, these little jaunts would be virtually impossible to make without being seen.

For one thing, Loch Ness is 50 feet above sea level. That means that anything entering or leaving the loch must pass through a system of seven locks. The locks are enclosures where the water can be raised or lowered, depending on which direction you're going. So Nessie would have to stop at each gate and wait to be let in. Since this has never happened, we must conclude that whatever might be in Loch Ness stays there—eating who knows what.

>> Nessie's Pu6licity Photos

In 1972 lawyer-scientist Robert Rines showed off the first of several snapshots and sonar tracings from Loch Ness. These images seem to show something large and decidedly beastlike swimming in the cold, murky waters of the loch.

Rines's underwater camera, equipped with a strobe light, captured pictures of a large flipper. And in 1976, Rines photographed what has come to be called the "gargoyle head."

If you were up on your dinosaur trivia, you'd probably say that the thing in Rines's rather spectacular photographs looks very much like a

Robert Rines's underwater camera captured this image of what could be a flipper in the murky waters of Loch Ness.

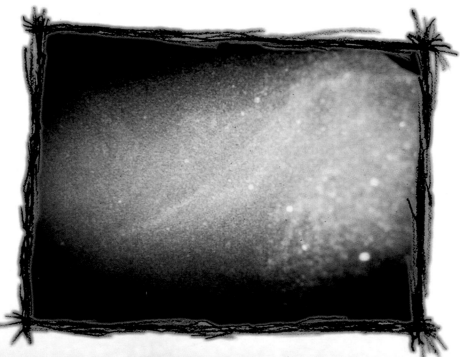

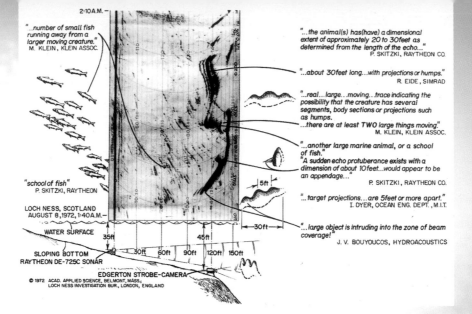

2:10 A.M. —

"..number of small fish running away from a larger moving creature."
M. KLEIN, KLEIN ASSOC.

"...the animal(s) has(have) a dimensional extent of approximately 20 to 30 feet as determined from the length of the echo..."
P. SKITZKI, RAYTHEON CO.

"...about 30 feet long...with projections or humps."
R. EIDE, SIMRAD

"...real...large...moving...trace indicating the possibility that the creature has several segments, body sections or projections such as humps."
...there are at least TWO large things moving."
M. KLEIN, KLEIN ASSOC.

"...another large marine animal, or a school of fish."
"A sudden echo protuberance exists with a dimension of about 10 feet...would appear to be an appendage..."
P. SKITZKI, RAYTHEON CO.

"school of fish"
P. SKITZKI, RAYTHEON

"...target projections...are 5 feet or more apart."
I. DYER, OCEAN ENG. DEPT., M.I.T.

5ft

LOCH NESS, SCOTLAND
AUGUST 8, 1972, 1:40 A.M. —

"...large object is intruding into the zone of beam coverage!"
J. V. BOUYOUCOS, HYDROACOUSTICS

30ft

WATER SURFACE
35ft   45ft

SLOPING BOTTOM
RAYTHEON DE-725C SONAR
30ft 60ft 90ft 120ft 150ft

EDGERTON STROBE-CAMERA
© 1972 ACAD. APPLIED SCIENCE, BELMONT, MASS.,
LOCH NESS INVESTIGATION BUR., LONDON, ENGLAND

Rines's sonar equipment used sound waves to locate objects in the loch in the way that bats use sonar to hunt prey. This sonar tracing shows the equipment's readings. Rines believed that the darker lines were proof of Nessie.

plesiosaur. Plesiosaurs were marine reptiles that inhabited the oceans when *T. rex* and his cousins were thundering around a swampy prehistoric Earth. But plesiosaurs have been extinct for tens of millions of years. So what could be in the loch?

If Rines has indeed captured a Nessie on film, this animal looks nothing at all like any creature alive today. Reptiles—even if they could grow to Nessie-like dimensions—could not survive in the loch's frigid waters, with its average temperature at an invigorating 42°F. Marine mammals, such as whales and dolphins, could—but they have to breathe air. Nessie surfaces, but not very often, and not for very long.

So what *did* Rines photograph? As things stand, nobody knows, and Nessie has declined to be interviewed. But if you go to Loch Ness, bring your camera. You may not get an autograph from our shy star, but you could come home with quite a story.

27

CHAPTER 3
I WALKED WITH A ZOMBIE

The studio bigwig shuffled some papers. "Giant lizards. No. Blobs of alien slime. No. Hairy, fanged, whatever these things are supposed to be. No! No! No! Lydia, give me an idea for a movie."

Lydia nibbled coyly on the pink eraser at the end of her number two pencil. "How about zombies?"

The studio bigwig blinked idiotically. "Eh?" Had he heard her right?

"The walking dead," said Lydia by way of explanation. "Cursed by *bokors* in voodoo rituals, buried, dug up, and turned into mindless slaves."

The studio bigwig continued to blink. "Cursed by bok—what did you call them?"

"Bokors. Evil voodoo priests."
"Hmmm," said the studio bigwig, rubbing his several chins. "Buried, huh? Are they dead?"
"They are the undead, sir."
"Right. You said that. Hey . . . are you making this up?"

"No, sir," said Lydia. "There are zombies in Haiti and other parts of the Caribbean, in Brazil, and in Louisiana. Or so I'm told," she added. "But people have seen them. They are unmistakable."

The studio bigwig scratched his bald head. "But how can these zombies be alive and dead at the same time?"

"Good question, sir," said Lydia. "How, indeed?"

>> The Undead, Take One

If you go to Haiti, you may hear this story. It is about a beautiful young woman from a wealthy family who caught the eye of a bokor. The bokor was amorous and attentive, but the woman rejected his advances. Angered and insulted, the vengeful bokor cast a spell on the woman. A few days later, she fell ill and died. After a brief wake, she was buried in the family plot.

Voodoo has its roots in West Africa, where it has been practiced for around 6,000 years. It came to Haiti *(above)* and the Caribbean region when African slaves were brought to the New World in the 1500s.

Four years passed. Then one day, a customer insisted she had seen the dead woman working as a slave in a local shop. But how could that be? Many people had attended the funeral. They had seen the poor woman lying dead in her coffin. They had watched the coffin lowered into the ground. Surely, this witness must be mistaken.

"No," she said, slowly shaking her head. "I saw the scar on her foot, from the burning candle that was overturned at her wake. I saw, too, how she shuffled, hunched over, from having been forced into a coffin that was too small for her."

Well, it was perfectly clear to most Haitians what had happened. The young woman had been turned into a zombie by the rejected bokor. Those who practice voodoo say that zombies can be created by powerful magic. With fearful words that invoke an evil, supernatural curse, the bokor removes the victim's soul and takes possession of it. The person then becomes little more than a body, capable of movement but not of free will, an empty shell that lacks a spirit. Without this essential presence, the victim appears to be dead, is declared so, and is buried. A short time later, the bokor slips into the grave-yard and causes the zombie to rise from the earth. Still flesh and blood but soul-less and enslaved, the zom-bie is now the living dead, surviving only to serve the bokor. It is certainly a terrible fate and one that is made worse because there are few escapes for the victim. Only by eating salt—or, in inland Haiti, being allowed to look upon the sea—can a zombie return to the grave and find release in true death.

HOLY TERRORS
Voodoo is a folk religion with deep roots in spirit beliefs and the occult. The Fon people of West Africa call it vodun, a word that means "godlike," or "that which is set apart and holy." The word zombie may come from the Bantu word nzambi. It, too, means "god." The reality could not be further from the truth.

Believers are terrified, not only of zombies but especially of being turned into one. There is no doubt in their minds that the walking dead do, indeed, exist. In fact, in places where voodoo is practiced, more than a few people say they have actually seen zombies. And zombie flesh, they may reveal to you, is sometimes sold in markets.

Well, now, this is quite a story. No wonder the makers of horror films found it so irresistible. But are we getting the entire story? Has something, perhaps, been left out?

>> The Undead, Take Two.
Pierre LeValle eyes the beautiful Marie from across the room. She is magnificent, he thinks, licking his chops like the big

Voodoo altars, such as the one above, often contain candles, money, food, and other offerings to the gods or to worshippers' ancestors. Skulls and other bones are sometimes used for protection against evil spirits.

bad wolf. But the beautiful Marie shows no interest in the evil bokor. Her dark eyes flash, and the bokor feels their burning fire. But it is not the heat of love, he realizes. It is the flame of hate, and he knows that she will never consent to be his bride. "Grrr," he says to himself, suddenly consumed with rage. "Grrr." But then he has an idea.

Just as the beautiful Marie has stolen his heart, so will he steal her soul. He is, after all, a voodoo priest, and if anybody knows how to whip up a little magic, it is he! He shall, he decides, turn the beautiful Marie into a zombie. If she would not be his wife willingly, then she shall be his slave!

Now, in the first filming of this scene, the bokor casts a spell on Marie, invoking very powerful magic to turn her into the aforementioned zombie.

But in this take, the camera is running in slow motion, allowing us to see what is really going on. Watch carefully. Notice that during the chanting and casting of spells, the bokor slips something into Marie's tea. You can bet it's not a lemon wedge.

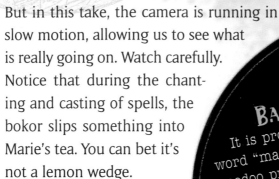

NOT EXACTLY BALLROOM DANCING

It is probably not coincidental that the word "mambo" refers to both a dance and a voodoo priestess. During the Haitian voodoo ritual, singing, dancing, and powerful drumming are used to call up the loa, spiritual ancestors that are African in origin but have come to be identified with the Catholic saints. As the drumming continues, ever faster and more furious, the loa take possession of the dancers, who then perform cures and give advice while in an ecstatic trance.

A Haitian woman reaches a trancelike state while performing a ritual voodoo dance.

The seeds of the thorn apple *(left)* are given to keep a victim in a trancelike state.

The bokor knows that belladonna, a plant also called deadly nightshade, contains atropine, a substance that can dilate the pupils and cause delirium and temporary paralysis. Then there is jimsonweed, also known as thorn apple. Like the deadly nightshade, jimsonweed contains natural chemicals that act like drugs. Its effects can include disorientation, confusion, slowed thinking, sluggishness, and indifference.

So let us now watch.

Unnoticed, the evil bokor has spiked the beautiful Marie's beverage of choice with a little deadly nightshade. As the atropine starts to take effect, Marie grows increasingly agitated. She becomes delirious, and her pupils begin to dilate. She stops sweating, and her saliva dries up. Her eyes, which can no longer blink, remain open. Her body, which can no longer move, appears as still as death.

Marie's family tries to rouse her, but they cannot. They grope for a pulse, but because the atropine affects the part of the brain that controls breathing and heartbeat, they feel nothing. "Dead!" they whisper—for indeed, that is exactly what it looks like. They hold a wake, and the following day, the beautiful Marie is buried alive.

Night falls, and a waning moon catches the dark shadow of a man beside Marie's freshly dug grave. It is the evil bokor, come to unearth his zombie slave. He sees that the effects of the belladonna have begun to wear off. Ah, good. Now he can give Marie the second drug—thorn apple. Regular doses of thorn apple will keep Marie sluggish and disinterested, disconnected and dull, and able to perform only the simplest of tasks. She will shuffle along, glassy-eyed and passive, and bound to the will of the bokor.

When it comes to zombies, what is real and what is legend? Are zombies real? Yes, in a way, they are. But if you don't know the chemical tricks, the line between science and sorcery will begin to blur, and you may find yourself believing in magic. So beware of half-truths and hidden ingredients. And don't drink any strange beverages.

CHAPTER 4
THE SWAMP THING
AND MOTHMAN

Premieres are always so exciting, especially for monster film buffs, and the fans are certainly gathered here tonight. Expected are Harlan Ford and Billy Mills, the gritty stars of *The Swamp Monster,* and Robbie Charbonnet, who plays the part of the Cajun guide. The film has gotten mixed reviews, but that hasn't stopped the thousands of screaming fans, who are anxious to judge for themselves.

Also tonight, we hope to catch a glimpse of the two couples Hollywood is all abuzz about: Roger and Linda Scarberry and Mary and Steve Mallette from *Mothman*. *Mothman* tells the story of a horrifying creature that skulks around West Virginia, scaring the daylights out of the citizens. Is it a real monster or is it . . . *something else?* In just a few moments, when the doors to the Rialto Theater finally open for our scary double feature, we'll all find out the spine-tingling truth.

The Swamp Monster

A swamp is never silent. It only seems that way. Maybe it's the Spanish moss hanging like stringy brown hair from the gnarled oak trees along the water's edge. Or the air, so thick and heavy that you'd swear you could spread it on cornbread. Or the alligators, whose watchful eyes break the water's surface without causing a ripple. Maybe it's the shadows.

A swamp can keep a secret, even from the locals. Just ask Harlan Ford and Billy Mills, who slogged into Louisiana's Honey Island Swamp one day to go hunting—and hightailed it out of there pretty darn fast when they found the wild boar and saw the tracks. Big tracks. The boar's throat had been sliced open, and its blood had run out onto the ground, where it lay in a pool, slowly gelling. That was in 1974.

They'd first seen the thing that made those tracks 11 years earlier. It had been standing right there in front of them, seven feet tall and hairy, its amber eyes glowing like a pair of headlights.

Harlan and Billy had frozen still that warm day in 1963. A moment later, the thing—whatever it was—took off, swallowed up by the cypress trees and buzzing insects.

Billy groped around for his voice. "Did you see that?" he squeaked.

Harlan pointed to a fresh set of tracks. "Look there." He bent down. "Three . . . no, wait. It looks like four toes, and the feet are webbed. Like a reptile."

Billy shook his head. "That was no reptile I've ever seen. Are we gonna tell anybody about this?"

Harlan stood up. "Now, what do you think?"

It was quite a tale that Harlan Ford and Billy Mills had carried out of the Honey Island Swamp that day. They'd seen . . . well, they didn't quite know what they'd seen. A monster of some kind, like Bigfoot, only different. Could they have been mistaken? Maybe it was just a 'gator, folks suggested.

"No! No way! Definitely not a 'gator!" They'd gone back later, they said, to make a cast of the prints, but it had rained, and the tracks had been washed out.

Harlan and Billy were not known to be pranksters, but nobody showed much interest in their swamp monster until 1974, when they came across the dead wild boar and the second set of tracks. That's when their story suddenly became good enough for TV, and Harlan found himself describing their experiences to millions of viewers on an episode of *In Search Of. . . .* After that, people started flocking to Louisiana, armed with everything from bags of plaster to 12-gauge shotguns, hoping to catch a glimpse of whatever it was. But only Harlan and a few of his buddies ever had any luck.

To Cajun swamp guide Robbie Charbonnet, it's no surprise that the swamp monster has only been seen by a handful of good buddies. With 45 years of swamp experience under his belt, he insists he's never once seen or heard anything he couldn't identify. Naturalist John Dennis also scoffs at the idea of an unknown animal hiding out in the swamp, as do most other experts in these matters. But Harlan Ford knew what he saw—or at least thought he saw—and until his death in 1980, he never gave up looking for it. Was he on a fool's errand or just putting on a good show for the tourists? The answer, of course, lies in the swamp.

>> Mothman

Seven miles outside of Point Pleasant, West Virginia, stands an old, abandoned explosives factory that once pumped out bombs for the Second World War. It is an eerie place, crisscrossed with miles of underground tunnels and dotted with squat concrete domes sealed with heavy steel doors. Tall, thick weeds fill in the gaps, providing hiding places for rabbits and other small animals, and deer meander through the spreading wildflowers. On hot summer nights, local kids challenge each other to drag races on the unpaved roads. But in late autumn, the area falls deeply silent, and the World War II ghosts are again left to themselves.

It was pretty late that night back in November 1966 when Roger and Linda Scarberry and their friends Mary and Steve Mallette drove through the property. But Roger had a hot '57 Chevy, and everyone was a little bored, and, well, you know. Roger gunned the Chevy and roared over the winding dirt roads, sending loose rocks flying. The shadows were deep and unbroken, the silence, thickly uncomfortable.

"Doesn't look like anybody's here tonight," said Linda. "Maybe we should go someplace else."

Roger pressed the brake and lazily threaded the Chevy around the domes, finally pulling up alongside the old generator plant, the engine idling. "So what do you think, guys," he began—but he never finished the sentence.

"Look!" Linda gasped.

Not far from the car, two small circles blazed bright red in the darkness.

"Oh, my gosh! What is it?" Mary screamed from the back seat.

40

"Aw, it's just an animal," said Steve, hugging his wife.

But no, it was not just an animal. As the thing raised its head, the foursome could see that the creature with the fiery eyes was a man—sort of. He was big—nearly seven feet tall—and dark gray. He stood there beside the abandoned generator plant, yards from the car, peering into the blackness, a pair of enormous wings folded against his broad back.

Nobody said a word. Nobody even breathed. All they could do was watch, spellbound, almost possessed by the creature's hypnotic eyes.

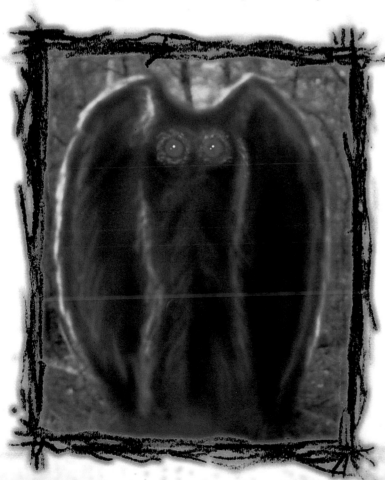

An artist's idea of Mothman

The man-thing slowly turned and lumbered off, like some hulking beast, toward the door of the plant.

"Let's get out of here!" Steve shouted.

Roger slammed the accelerator to the floor, and the Chevy burst forward. Within seconds, they were off the dirt road and heading for Route 62, mute with fear, their hearts thundering in their chests.

"Roger!" Linda shrieked.

"I know. I see it!"

They all saw it, standing on a small rise, tremendous, menacing, its leathery wings spread wide like some horror from a Dracula movie. The thing had reappeared, or maybe it was another one, a second one! Roger's knuckles were white on the steering wheel, his right foot pressed hard against the floorboard. The speedometer read 90.

As the Chevy roared past, the creature lifted straight up off the ground and began to follow the car, its massive wings outstretched but motionless. Roger was doing almost 100 miles an hour when he reached the Point Pleasant city limits, but the creature kept pace. And then, just like that, it was gone.

Still shaking, Roger, his wife, and the Mallettes jumped out of the car, barreled up the steps of the Mason County Courthouse, burst through the door, and breathlessly spilled their story to Deputy Millard Halstead. Halstead listened patiently, looked at the time, and arched an eyebrow.

"I swear, Millard," said Roger. "I swear that's what we saw." He ran his fingers through his hair. "I know it sounds crazy, but...." His voice trailed off.

Halstead nodded. He'd known these kids since they were born. They were okay, good kids, not taken to pulling stupid pranks. He grabbed the keys to the prowler. "Let's go," he said. "Let's take a look."

They returned to the site but found no sign of the creature.

"Millard. . . ."

Halstead patted Roger's shoulder. "I believe you, kid," he said. "We'll look into it tomorrow."

The following day, Sheriff George Johnson called a press conference, and after interviewing the two couples, reporter

MOTHMAN, OR *TYTO ALBA*?

The shaken witnesses said that it had glowing red eyes. "It was shaped like a man, but bigger" and "it had big wings folded against its back," said one. "It was grayish," said another, "and walked on sturdy legs with a shuffling gait." Others said, "It squeaked like a big mouse." Or, "It was definitely a bird." Most said it was headless, with red eyes set in the upper part of its body. One woman saw "a funny little face" but no beak. And from 70 miles north of the original sightings came reports of a gigantic bird with a 10-foot wingspan and "two big eyes, like automobile reflectors."

What a fearsome creature! What a horror from the depths of the night! Or maybe not. Allowing for some exaggeration by witnesses, could Mothman actually be *Tyto alba*, the common barn owl? This elusive bird has a heart-shaped face, glowing eyes, and a short neck that makes it seem as if its head is in its chest. When it takes flight, with a magnificent 44-inch wingspan, it looks enormous. And instead of the familiar hoot we think of, the barn owl's cry is more like a soft hiss or, sometimes, the squeak of a mouse. . . .

Mary Hyre sent the story out over the Associated Press wire service. By nightfall, everybody was talking about the mysterious winged creature. By morning, it had a name: Mothman.

The Mothman sightings continued throughout November. One after the other, sane and sober witnesses came forward with unbelievable tales of their encounters. Connie Carpenter said she nearly went into a ditch when she spotted Mothman standing on the side of the road one morning. Its red eyes were characteristically ablaze, and its 10-foot wings were stretched wide, giving it the appearance of some giant prehistoric bird. Connie watched in horror as it rose straight up, hovered several feet above the ground, and headed directly for her car. Panicked, she slammed her foot on the accelerator, doing 90 most of the way home. Volunteer firemen Paul Yoder and Benjamin Enochs also saw Mothman, as did several teenagers and an elderly gentleman who claimed he had found the creature camped out on his front lawn.

Well, this is just about as weird as it gets. Common sense tells us to dismiss the whole thing as utter nonsense. But *something* must have triggered all those sightings. What could it have been?

The film ends, and the house lights come up. The audience stirs, and a moment later it is oozing out of the aisles and flowing upstream toward the huge double doors. You watch the credits unroll on the flickering screen until all the monsters have faded to black. Then, just to be on the safe side, you check under your seat. Nothing's there, of course. Monsters can't survive in the harsh glare of the movie theater's tacky chandeliers. *Most of them* have gone back to celluloid sleep, dreaming Bigfoot and Mothman dreams until they are roused to wakefulness by the projector. As for the rest, maybe they're—hey, up there, in the balcony . . . did you just hear something?

Books// Coleman, Loren, and Jerome Clark. *Cryptozoology A to Z: The Encyclopedia of Loch Monsters, Sasquatch, Chupacabras, and Other Authentic Mysteries of Nature.* New York: Simon & Schuster, 1999.
This source offers profiles of more than 100 unexplained creatures—from the Abominable Snowman to the Zuiyo-maru Monster—who may or may not really be out there.

Innes, Brian. *Giant Humanlike Beasts.* Austin, TX: Raintree Steck-Vaughn, 1999.
This book takes a look at the mystery surrounding Bigfoot, Yeti, and other unidentified monsters. Presenting a range of background information, from ancient tales to modern evidence, the book invites readers to draw their own conclusions.

Videos// *The Beast of Loch Ness.* PBS, 1999.
This video from the science show *NOVA* examines the Loch Ness legend from the viewpoints of both believers and nonbelievers. Famous Nessie hunters such as Robert Rines take part, along with more skeptical observers. You can also check out a related website at <http://www.pbs.org/wgbh/nova/lochness>.

White Zombie. United Artists, 1932.
This hokey, old horror film tells the story of a young couple who cross paths with a rather creepy man in Haiti. The man, Murder Legendre, turns out to be a powerful zombie master, and lots of spookiness follows. Considered by many to be the first zombie movie, the film has been released in new VHS and DVD editions.

We6sites// *Skeptiseum*
<http://www.skeptiseum.org>
This website, from the Committee for the Scientific Investigation of Claims of the Paranormal (CSICOP), is an on-line museum of the paranormal—presented with a skeptical edge. It takes a look at the claims, evidence, and possible holes in the stories of all kinds of out-of-the-ordinary phenomena, including a few monsters. CSICOP also takes on the Honey Island Swamp Monster at <http://www.csicop.org/si/2001-07/i-files.html> and Mothman at <http://www.csicop.org/list/listarchive/msg00317.html>.

Abominable Snowman. *See* Bigfoot

belladonna, 34, 35
Bigfoot, 5–17; description, 7, 9–10,
    11–12; footprints, 8–9, 11, 16–17;
    habitat, 7, 11; skepticism, 6–7, 9–10,
    14
bokors, 29–35

Campbell, Alex, 20

Darwin, Charles, 13
deadly nightshade. *See* belladonna
Dinsdale, Tim, 22–23

Ford, Harlan, 36–39

Gigantopithecus, 14–15
Gray, Hugh, 18–19

Haiti, 29–31, 33
Honey Island Swamp, 37–39
Howard-Bury, Lieutenant Colonel C. K.,
    8–11

Loch Ness Monster, 18–27; description,
    18–19, 20, 23; habitat, 24–25;
    skepticism, 19, 21–22, 23, 24–25,
    27

Mills, Billy, 36–39
Mothman, 40–45; description, 41, 44,
    45; skepticism, 44

Nessie. *See* Loch Ness Monster

Patterson, Roger, 5–7, 11
plesiosaur, 26–27

Rines, Richard, 26–27

Sasquatch. *See* Bigfoot
Scotland, 18–27
skepticism and skeptics, 6–7, 9–10, 14,
    19, 21–22, 23, 24–25, 27, 34, 35,
    38, 39, 44
Surgeon's Photograph, 20–22
Swamp Monster, 36–39; description,
    37; skepticism, 38, 39

thorn apple, 34, 35
Tibet, 8–11

voodoo, 29–31; origins, 30, 31;
    practices, 32, 33. *See also* Haiti

Yeti. *See* Bigfoot

zombies, 28–35; description, 29,
    30–31, 34–35; skepticism, 34, 35.
    See also belladonna, *bokors,* Haiti,
    thorn apple

>> About the Author

Born in Baltimore, Maryland, Judith Herbst grew up in Queens, New York, where she learned to jump double Dutch with amazing skill. She has since lost that ability. A former English teacher, she ran away from school in her tenure year to become a writer. Her first book for kids was *Sky Above and Worlds Beyond,* whose title, she admits, was much too long. She loves to write and would rather be published, she says, than be rich, which has turned out to be the case. Herbst spends summers in Maine on a lake with her cats and laptop.

>> Photo Acknowledgments

Photographs and illustrations in this book are used with the permission of: René Dahinden/Fortean Picture Library, pp. 6 (all), 7 (both), 11; Cliff Crook/Fortean Picture Library, pp. 8, 16, 17; Richard Svensson/Fortean Picture Library, p. 9; Tony Healy/Fortean Picture Library, pp. 12, 20; American Philosophical Society, p. 13; © Mark Erdmann, p. 15; Fortean Picture Library, pp. 19, 21, 32, 33; © Tim Dinsdale, p. 22 (all); © R. H. Rines/Academy of Applied Science, pp. 26, 27; Raymond Buckland/Fortean Picture Library, p. 30; Dr. Elmar R. Gruber/Fortean Picture Library, p. 34; William M. Rebsamen/Fortean Picture Library, p. 41. Illustrations by Bill Hauser, pp. 4–5, 14, 18, 28, 35, 36, 38–39, 42–43.

Cover photos by: Fortean Picture Library (top), René Dahinden/Fortean Picture Library (bottom).